Seasons Come and Go, But God Never Changes

Gracia Kasanda Mubala

 A catalogue record for this book is available from the National Library of Australia

Copyright © 2020 Gracia Kasanda Mubala
All rights reserved.
ISBN: 978-1-922343-39-0

Linellen Press
265 Boomerang Road
Oldbury, Western Australia
www.linellenpress.com.au

Dedication

I dedicate this book to The Kasanda's family for the labour put into ministry for the glory of God

Contents

Dedication iii

Contents v

Acknowledgments vii

Introduction 1

Chapter 1 4

Different seasons of life 4

Chapter 2 8

The Best Season? 8

Chapter 3 13

How to Discover your Purpose 13

Chapter 4 21

Change of Season 21

Conclusion 23

About the Author 24

Acknowledgments

I would like to acknowledge my parents, Pastor Luc Kasanda and Pauline, for raising and training me. To my wonderful husband, thank you for believing in me. I would like also to acknowledge my mentor pastor Anette Dei along with my current spiritual father Apostle Isaiah Maji for allowing God to use them to teach and mostly help me discover who I really am and align myself with God's calling upon my life.

I dedicate this book to the youth and young mothers out there as they journey in different seasons of life and experiences. I pray that the information in this book will set you on the right path to discover your purpose so you can live a quality life in every season of your life.

Introduction

On 21st April, two days after my second daughter's birthday, I had a really good sleep. But as a mum of toddlers, my sleep system in this season differs from everyone else. I woke up around 2.00 am with the song below in my mind.

>   C   F   C   G   C
>
> (Seasons, come), seasons come, seasons go oh oh, they come and go   X2
>
> Problems come problems go, they come and go
>
> *Chorus*
>
>   C   F   C   G C   F
>
> But He never changes, He is the same Jesus, the Rock of Ages
>
> C   C   G
>
> He is the same Messiah, ah, ah, ah

I learnt this song from a church member who later became a very close friend. She joined the church soon after my father started his own ministry in Australia. She was more than a friend at the time. But little did I know that this friendship was just for a season. When my father started his ministry, my family and I joined hands with him. For me, this was a season of hard work for my family.

When we were in Zambia, my siblings and I were very young, and the church was well-established. So, for me, church was just fun. But on coming to Australia, it changed from fun to labour. Until you move to a different season in life, you may not appreciate those in that season. For example, most ladies will agree that, until they became mothers, they didn't really understand and sometimes didn't appreciate their mother.

When my father opened a church, my sisters and I were automatically in the choir. I started leading prayers, doing administration work, and many other things. For us, this was a season of training in ministry. In the beginning, it was hard, but the Lord was and still is sending people to help, encourage, and support us to carry His work forward.

A good example was the sister who taught us the song. In each season, when a person's agenda that God sent them to accomplish in their life is fulfilled, let them go. Otherwise, it will turn into hurt, disappointment, and destroy the relationship and the fond memories of being together. And that's what I've learnt throughout the seasons. Sometimes we want to keep people near us because we feel guilty of letting them go. We think of all the things they did for us. But the truth is that, if God doesn't use a person to help you, that help will have strings attached. For example, you will hear statements like: "After all I did for you, this is how you repay me?" even when you do not mean to be evil.

Chapter 1
Different seasons of life

Each season in life requires Wisdom and Courage! I am not talking about the seasons of the year such as summer, winter, autumn, and spring. I am talking about the happy, sad, doubt, and seasons of certainty that come and go. As you are reading this book, I am certain you are all in different seasons of your lives. Each season of life comes with its easy and difficult assignment(s). For example, the hard assignment when my father started ministry in Australia was the awareness of Australian culture as we were still new to Australia; my sisters and I were still in school and had part-time jobs, and our parents were well involved in the community so we were everywhere! It felt like the season would never end, but whenever the church sister sung her song, it would comfort me. Indeed, seasons come and go! According to Ecclesiastes 3:1, there's a time for everything.

Have you ever examined yourself after going through a season or while in a certain season of your life? Have you ever traced the effects that season left on you?

As these seasons come and go, they make us stronger, wiser, and may change us for the better – some for the worst. The only person who remains the same season in and season out is God Almighty! Just like a phone needs a power source for charging and a car needs fuel or a petrol station for refuelling, we also need a power source to get the wisdom to make the right decisions, draw strength to bring us through the seasons. He is our Power source.

This book aims to help you to have a positive attitude in every season you might find yourself in in life.

Our lives here on earth are valued by the quality of the seasons in and out. Some people however choose to give up when they are going through a difficult time.

I was privileged to meet my mentor in the season where everything was on a standstill. One day during our Bible study, she posed me a question. She said, "Gracia, can you define yourself?"

Full of confidence, I mentioned all the titles and roles I thought defined me. She acknowledged this, and then asked me that, if all the things that defined me were taken away, who would I think I was? Mmm, it felt like an exam!

The point I am trying to make here is that sometimes we allow the seasons to define us.

I am a mother of young children. When I'm asked who I am, I simply answer "I am a mum."

But who will you be when the children grow up and leave? Who are you when that voice is taken away? A singer?

Many of us want to live long on earth. There's nothing wrong with that, but the thing is, it's not about *how long* we live, it's *how well* we live our lives. The quality of life matters because the reality is, when a person dies, he or she will be remembered for what he or she did on earth and how many lives he or she has touched. It is by God's grace that we have what we have, and the years we live on earth are also by the Grace of God. Therefore, it's important to know who we are.

When we discover who we are, we can avoid living a careless life. The variables in our lives will not define who we are as we transit in different seasons of life. My mentor guided me to defining myself. Variables are things that change, such as friends and jobs, just to mention a few. On the other hand, the constants are things that don't change. Who are you when that house or car is taken away from you?

When you get the revelation of who you are, you can go through any season.

My mentor helped me realise that if the variables like cars, houses or even when my children were to be taken away from me, I would still be who I am, the temple of the Holy Ghost. Sounds nice, right?

Yes, it is nice. Every one of us will give an account of every moment of time we wasted here on earth. Ouch! God is the only one who never dies and never changes, season in season out.

Living a quality life can only be achieved when you know your purpose on earth. When you know your purpose here on earth, then you can set a vision for your life, and a mission and objective to achieve that vision. Sounds like a business, right?

Yes, for me, life should have a structure. As a person, I have system in place to do things. For example, God created the garden before He made man. It becomes easier when you know who you are and your purpose on earth. During the season when my parents decided to open a church, I was given some responsibilities in the church because first I love God and second, I was good at them. However, it seemed like a burden to me because during that season, I was not aware of who I really was or my purpose under the sun.

Chapter 2
The Best Season?

In order for a person to get through the seasons in life without feeling it's a burden, we have to know that there's a season for everything, and everyone. In the book of Acts Chapter 6, the apostles were sure of what they needed to do. It's about the seasons: Calling & Season. Just because I'm called to do something doesn't mean I have to do it right now, for it may not be the season. Even if a particular thing needs to be done doesn't mean that I have to do it.

There certain people who come into our lives for a season. Call them friends, teachers, work colleagues, even church mates. This is because God had predestined each and every one of us, where we would be, when and for what reason. God is all-knowing and has time and seasons in His hands.

Seasons come and season go. It is in a difficult season that our integrity is tested. Each season in a person's life contributes to shaping character; resisting the storms of life and so on. Each season changes us to be happier or sad. The only one that is not changed is God. He never changes, He is the same yesterday, today and forever more! That's why having Him on your side in each season will make you triumph.

My current spiritual father Apostle Isaiah Maji said to the congregation:

"until you know who you are, you will remain a stranger to yourself, family and environment. When a person knows who he or she is, his or her stimulant, then he or she will know the proper way to respond or the right action to take."

Knowing who you are will help you not to lose your integrity for God because of the season you go through in life. Some lose the integrity of their calling because life becomes too hard or too easy. Knowing who you are in each season and having a pure relationship with God will get you through and prove you trust worthy.

The best season in life is when you discover who you are!

For young people, when you discover who you are, negative company will not easily influence you. For those with low self-esteem, when you discover who you are, the stress of pleasing anyone and trying to be someone you are not will be eliminated. There are young people who end up pregnant without planning for it because they don't know who they are – they have no vision in life and don't even know why they exist. There are many factors that contribute to that. But this book emphasises that if you know who are, you can be productive in each season of your life.

> **If Jesus was not vision focused,**
> **He wouldn't stand up for himself.**

The story of Jesus standing up for Himself is in John 7-5

"⁴ No one who wants to become a public figure acts in secret. Since you are doing these things, show yourself to the world.

⁵ For even his own brothers did not believe in him."

The main problem here was not for Jesus to perform miracles in public. The main issue was that His brothers didn't believe in Him!

If I were Jesus, I was either going to ask them that: "Did I tell you that I want to be a public figure? Or prove to them that I can do it in public just like I do it in secret?"

But because Jesus knew who He was, He was not persuaded by their imposition. Rather, He had the wisdom and courage to do the right thing in the season because he was confident in who He was. The best thing for Him was to stay behind as His brothers went to the festival and went in His own time. It's easier to be tempted to shine faster, but when it's not the season you can only wait when you know who you are, and when you know it's your season to shine. But without spending quality time with God it's easy to be distracted.

Many of us are called, but is it the appointed season to start ministry? Many of the young ladies can't wait to be in a relationship because all their friends are wearing the expensive ring and are enjoying life. Some even enter relationships too early and later can't bear the weight that comes with being in those relationships. Entering a season before the time is right can ruin your chances before your time. But thank God for God.

I would like to take this opportunity to ask anyone who feels that they have lost it in life because of a mistake they made in a particular season in their life. As you read this passage, I want to ask you to give your life to the Lord Jesus Christ. Come back if you have backslid because God is good. He can and will restore your life and set you to enjoy seasons of your life! Joel 2:25

Chapter 3
How to Discover your Purpose

Discovering your purpose is a good foundation to navigate through life and its seasons. The dictionary definition of 'purpose' is: the reason for which something is done or created or for which something exists. A 'calling' is a strong desire to a particular way of life or career. Purpose and calling interact. God said to Jeremiah:

"I knew you before I formed you in your mother's womb. Before you were born, I set you apart and appointed you as my prophet to the nations." Jeremiah 1:5.

Every one of us was born for a reason. Have you ever wondered which season were you born into your family? Was it a time of dryness that you brought joy? Or have you ever met someone who told you that you came at the right time!

There's a reason why you were born into that family, country, moved to another country etc. – a purpose is a purpose.

There's nothing like a big or small calling. Yes, some callings have higher demands than others but are all-important for the human race and our environment. Purpose is not singular but is connected to:

1. Family
2. Community and
3. Ministry.

So, whatever your purpose is take it seriously and set out objectives to carry out your purpose. For me, Vision, goals and actions prove that I am a woman of assignment. I do pray in the morning, asking God to help me achieve my purpose for the day, whether it's putting a smile on someone's face or whatever I need to achieve.

When I was a teenager, I couldn't wait to finish university so I could get married and at least have the freedom to express myself. Can I get a witness somebody? Please don't get me wrong on this one. This is not true for everyone. But thank God that generations are changing. Some parents can still allow their children to truly express themselves before they are corrected and disciplined. The point I am trying to make is that I couldn't wait to start expressing the vision I had for my life. For me it seemed like once I was married, then at least I wouldn't be fully controlled. I didn't know that my purpose here on earth was what I wanted to express.

Again, the best season in a person's life is when you discover who you are! Some people get to find out who they are or their purpose earlier in life, some later. That is why this book is written. When you find out your purpose, you can focus on maximising your potential in each season of your life. Also, purpose can grow, depending on how well one handles it. Below is something I just copied and pasted from my old notes, not knowing then that I would ever write a book for sharing.

As human beings, we need to know that, no matter how anointed we can be, time doesn't wait for anyone. That is why John walked with the assurance of who he was and worked with time. There was a time he lived with his parents, a time he moved to the wilderness and a time for ministry.

Below is an example of how I began to find out my purpose – it might help you do yours.

8/11/2019: *Why am I needed in this season*:

Family - *Channel for my family's deliverance (Father. Mother, 2 sisters, brother and my in-laws).*

Be a mum and a wife (By being an obedient daughter of the Holy Ghost

Church/ ministry-Intercede for Siloam Gospel ministry & organize worship team and music in Jesus Prayer and Power Ministry, Perth.

We all have a general purpose. For instance, as Christians we are a chosen generation, royal priesthood, children of God adopted into, etc. Then we have specific purposes or calling individually because purpose and calling interact. "For He will be great in the sight of the Lord". When the angel of God came to Zachariah, he specified who John the Baptist would be to Zachariah and Elizabeth-Family and community (Luke 1:13-15).

"He will be a joy and delight to you, and many will rejoice because of his birth, he shall never take wine or strong drink, and he will be filled with the Holy Spirit even from his mother's womb"

The best thing about knowing your purpose or calling is that you will not waste time on unnecessary things but rather focus on maximising on your purpose. The perfect example here is in Galatians 1:14-15.

"I was far ahead of my fellow Jews in my zeal for the traditions of my ancestors. But even before I was born, God chose me and called me by his marvellous grace. Then it pleased him."

When Paul was distorted of his God-sent purpose here on earth, he wasted his time on Judaism traditions. But when he knew the plan of God, he focused and produced quality work of his purpose.

How do I discover my Purpose/Calling?

First of all, I would like to use Paul's example in Galatians 1:14 and 15. Paul said he was extremely zealous for the traditions of my fathers (NIV translation), he was advancing (English standard version). Paul, then Saul, was zealous and advancing what he was not created for because, he was not in a relationship with his creator.

1. Relationship with your Creator.

From this discovery, the first step for one to discover his or her purpose is by starting a personal relationship with your creator. When I started quiet time on a regular basis in 2018 November, December, I started to discover myself through God. My stress level began to decrease because I discovered that the season I was in was not for me to work but I am a compulsory mentor to my girls. Before I discovered this, I became stressed because I really wanted to go to work, and was pressured by my parents and others around me to do so. I tried my best that I even went back to school after completing my Bachelor Degree.

During that time, something was saying inside of me, I'm speaking like I used to before I started discovering that the Holy Ghost was residing in me. It used to say to me: this is the time to lay a foundation with a one-on-one relationship with my children because when this season is passed, I will just be checking on them. That settled me for a bit until the 9th March 2020.

We were at Bible Study that Tuesday night when Apostle Isaiah Maji taught us about prophecy and asked us to exercise our gift. Then the sister I was paired with spoke to me about how God knows that I have put my goals on hold and work with His plan to stay home with the children, and because of that, there'll be a time He'll come through for my children. Oh! It still hits me hard because I know the battles I fought in my mind.

What the sister said goes along with the word of encouragement my husband, Jean Jacques, had said to me the day before. My husband saw the job applications I had made the previous night. So, he was encouraging me that God had given us beautiful children, if I could just focus on laying a good foundation I would not regret it. And moreover, it was about the matter of time (one year) that I could go back to work or choose to study again.

God is faithful in any season and at any time. Having a relationship with Him and allowing Him to be part of your life is the best way to discover your purpose and He'll assure you that He is with you all the time so you can carry on with your purpose.

2. **Another way to discover your purpose**

is through passions, dreams and confirmation through prophecy. These are just a few for there is no specific way for all of us, but knowing the mind of God through a relationship with Him prevails. Then He can speak to you through His prophets, in your dreams, through His word and so on.

Chapter 4
Change of Season

As seasons change, so as our life circumnutates, friendships and even environment changes. Changes in our life seasons are also good indicators of what is required of us. For example, John the Baptist knew why he was born. There was a time he stayed with his parents, moved to the wilderness for a while and then entered a season to baptise people. John knew who he was and understood his seasonal assignments. When you start to understand your purpose, your season will start to look green even when it's a dry season in your life. It will help you focus on the important things and before you know it, you will transit into another season.

John Ch9:4-5 Jesus takes seasons & times.

Discern time to complete assignment in each season is very important. As you complete each season assignment, you will not have to go back and forth over certain things.

John 10:36-Jesus.

When you know your purpose/calling, you can put your enemies in their place.

In every season of life, our time is not God's time. Don't put strings on God. It's important to remain in strong connection with God because whenever something is about to birth, there's always a pharaoh released to abort. So, stand in the gap and pray against every pharaoh that has been released. Seasons are good times, tough times, labour and harvest seasons. In every season, the enemy will bring a counterfeit purpose especially when you don't align yourself with the presence of God.

Conclusion

Knowing who you are can reduce the stress level in each season of your life you get to traverse.

When you discover your purpose, you can focus on maximising your potential in each season of your life.

Knowing your purpose can allow you to stand your ground when the enemy attacks.

Lastly, by maximising your purpose, God can increase it.

References

The Holy Bible books
Google Dictionary

About the Author

Originally from Congo DR, Gracia moved from Zambia to Australia in 2006. Gracia is the mother of three beautiful children who, with her husband, devotes her time to the family and the ministry. Having grown up as a pastor's daughter, she maintains important family values and strong relationships with her children, while serving the ministry and the Lord.

In Church, Gracia sings in the choir and plays the Keyboard. She has studied Commerce, Counselling and Community Services, which enabled her to write this, her second, book.

Gracia is also the author of *Ministry and Parenting Challenges*.

www.ingramcontent.com/pod-product-compliance
Lightning Source LLC
Chambersburg PA
CBHW071550080526
44588CB00011B/1861